a LEISURE-PLAN book in colour

shrubs for all seasons

ANN BONAR, B.Sc. (Hort.)

contents

Leisure-Plan books in colour are for pleasure and better living — the special kind of pleasure which comes from success with a rewarding hobby or pastime.

Authoritative, lively, packed with up-to-date information, these books can be built into a library for the whole family.

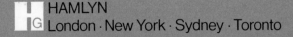

HAMLYN
London · New York · Sydney · Toronto

Front cover: *Clematis* Nelly Moser   Back cover: *Camellia japonica elegans*

shrubs and garden design

There are many things for which the Victorians are accountable, and one of them is the legacy of dark, dank, unhappy dripping shrubs clustered gloomily round the front door, effectively cutting off sunshine and air, and serving as a launching pad for spiders and beetles *en route* to the interior of the house.

Another picture often conjured up by the word 'shrubs' is of a stunted and dusty little collection of bushes, much too close together, with occasional, rather insipid-looking flowers at the ends of long, thin stems, appearing at rare intervals throughout the summer.

Advantages of shrubs

Nothing could be further from the real picture. In fact, shrubs are amongst the most beautiful garden plants that there are. The flowers of many are of special beauty with attractive colouring and, often, distinctive shape. Many, too, have delightful scent. It is perfectly possible to have shrubs in flower all the year round, from January to December, even in a small garden.

Leaf colouring

A good many shrubs have a bonus, or additional merit, besides flowers. One of these is the colour that the leaves of various kinds turn before leaf-fall. The reds, oranges, yellows and intermediate shades between them, taken on by the foliage in autumn, are as colourfully

satisfying as any of the hues of their flowers.

In addition to autumn colouring, there are shrubs with permanent leaves, that is, the evergreens, whose leaves may be plain green, sprinkled with yellow or streaked with white, they may be 'evergrey', with grey, silvery or grey-green leaves – these sorts are extremely useful, either in their own right, or as foils for other plants – or they may be blotched with purple or pink, as *Salvia officinalis purpurascens* and *Parthenocissus henryana* are.

Fruits

Then, too, there are the berries and fruits. The large, golden quinces of japonica, the bright red berries of cotoneaster, the red and black fruits of viburnum species, and the long smoky-blue pods of *Decaisnea fargesii* are just a few examples of how wide-ranging the colours of fruits are, to say nothing of the interesting and varied shapes they can be. In addition they may last from autumn into and through the winter, and still be on the plant when the new season's leaves or flowers start to unfold.

Scent

Scent is another shrubby virtue and can vary

(Right)
Mixed plantings of shrubs and selected bedding plants or perennials can be extremely effective and make good use of the space available

from the heavy aroma of the syringa and the Mexican orange blossom, choisya, and the mock orange, philadelphus, almost soporific in their strength, through the less-powerful honeysuckles and lavender to the lighter and more elusive ones of buddleia and cytisus.

Along with these obvious merits of colour, scent and beauty of form, shrubs have practical assets too. Provided one or two golden rules of planting are remembered, they will thrive for many years with a good deal less attention than a herbaceous border or rock garden would require; moreover, plant for plant they will cover considerably more ground. A good start, attention to pruning, regular mulching and an occasional application of a concentrated fertiliser (depending on the soil), are mostly all that will have to be done; bugs and blights, that is, pests and diseases, are few, while there is the pleasure, over many years, of watching the shrub grow bigger and more beautiful.

GARDEN DESIGN

The use of shrubs in the garden is an essential part of the overall garden arrangement of plants; they give it the skeleton, so to speak, on which the flesh in the form of alpines, bulbs and herbaceous plants is hung. Used in groups, they can contrast or blend with one another in the colour of flower, habit of growth and the shape of leaf.

As individual specimens, it is possible to enjoy the 'personality' of each shrub even more. Where a specimen shrub is required it is wise to choose one which has as many good points as possible, that is flowers in spring or summer, followed by berries, and evergreen leaves, or, if the shrub is deciduous, a distinctive shape in winter. Specimens are set off to the best advantage when they are planted in a lawn, but a small bed should be cut out round them for the first few years until they are established, so the grass and shrub roots are not foraging for food in the same area.

Uses of shrubs

In borders, shrubs can harmonise with herbaceous perennials, annuals and bedding plants very well, thus providing the modern mixed border, rather than the older type of purely herbaceous border. It is surprising, and highly satisfactory, to see the plant 'pictures' which can be obtained by blending these different kinds of plants. With care and forethought it is possible to have one of these plant pictures reaching its most attractive stage as the one next to it is beginning to fade. Tall-growing, fastigiate shrubs can be used as 'exclamation marks' in various parts of the garden, to draw attention to a particular planting nearby, or to lead one's eye to a view beyond it. Climbing shrubs help immeasurably to extend the range of a garden, since it is possible to make use of another plane by planting against walls, fences, or over dead tree stumps, and encouraging the plants to ramble over them.

Shrubs will help to block one part of the garden off from another, thus creating the 'surprise' effect which makes any good garden. To come unexpectedly on a new part, however small, which is otherwise hidden from sight, makes the garden very much more interesting and attractive. A little space enclosed by shrubs will be sheltered and pleasant to sit in, and will provide a home for tender plants.

(Opposite page)
Phlomis fruticosa offers both yellow, hooded flowers in summer and 'evergrey' felted leaves

(Top right)
The winter-flowering ***Jasminum nudiflorum***, with its bright yellow, scented flowers, is one of the joys of the garden from mid-November

(Bottom right)
Pyracantha varieties follow their hawthorn-like flowers with fiery red, bright orange or yellow berries

(Top)
The useful and decorative *Cotoneaster horizontalis*, aptly named the fishbone cotoneaster, often bears its berries from autumn until almost the end of the winter season

(Bottom)
This splendid planting, which combines the opposite virtues of restfulness and quiet stimulation, includes ericas, hebes, and the lovely *Chamaecyparis pisifera plumosa nana*

(Top)
There is a special richness about the autumn display of *Viburnum opulus* Notcutt's Variety, both from the leaves and the translucent berries

(Bottom)
The syringas, or lilacs, are some of the best-loved shrubs of spring, their scent and beauty being ample compensation for the relatively short flowering season

(Right)
Shrubs can be used to separate one part of the garden from the other, thus achieving the element of surprise which is always desirable

shrubs for spring and summer

The shrubs described here and in the following chapter make up only a small part of the tremendous variety available today. They all have an outstanding merit of one kind or another, such as flowers, leaves, fruit, unusual time of flowering – sometimes they have more than one attraction – and all, with a few exceptions which are noted in the individual descriptions, are easy to grow.

SPRING-FLOWERING SHRUBS
Azalea see Rhododendron.

Berberis Deciduous or evergreen shrubs, the barberries are not only embarrassingly prolific with their flowers, but frequently also have most attractive foliage or berries. They could be said to take the place of rhododendrons in gardens with limy soil, flowering at the same time of the year, namely from March to June. They will, however, grow well in any soil; the deciduous species do well in a sunny position and the evergreens in sun or partial shade. *Berberis darwinii*, 8–10 ft., produces deep orange-yellow flowers in April, to be followed later by blue berries; it is evergreen. *B. linearifolia* is also evergreen and has most lovely apricot-coloured flowers – the berries are blue-black. It is low growing, to 3–4 ft. *B. stenophylla*, another evergreen, has bright golden flowers in sprays during April, grows vigorously to 10 ft., and has dark blue berries. A deciduous barberry with several

bonuses is *B. thunbergii atropurpurea*, which has purple leaves and yellow flowers; it grows to about 4 ft. tall with bright red berries and even more brilliant foliage in the autumn. Prune all these, if necessary, immediately after flowering, cutting back flowered shoots to new growth, but remember this removes potential berries and may make the plant too vigorous in growth.

Camellia Tea, and the decorative camellia, share the same genus of plants – *Camellia sinensis* is the tea plant, and *C. japonica* and its varieties are those usually grown for ornamental purposes. One of the camellia's charms is the variation in the form of flower, which may be single, double, fimbriated, the anemone type, peony-centred, and so on. Camellias do best in slightly sheltered positions with acid or neutral soil – if grown in chalky soils they need special treatment (see page 57). The soil should contain peat and/or leafmould; mulch them in spring and autumn and feed in spring with a sprinkling of a slow-acting organic fertiliser. Height varies from about 6–12 ft., but up to 30 ft. is possible, and virtually no pruning is required. Some good varieties are: Adolphe Audusson, dark red, semi-double; Contessa Lavinia Maggi, white, striped red, double; Destiny, pink and white striped, semi-double; Donation, pink, semi-double; *donckelarii,* dark red, white variegation, semi-double; J. C. Williams, shell-pink, single; and *mathotiana alba,* a pure white, double variety.

Ceanothus Only one variety of ceanothus is given here, blue-flowered Cascade, which is evergreen and lives up to its name. For further details of ceanothus, see under autumn-flowering shrubs, page 22.

Chaenomeles A shrub whose vermilion, buttercup-shaped flowers have a cluster of golden stamens in the centre of each, the japonica (to give its common name) blooms in March-April, but sometimes produces the occasional flower in February. It is hardy, rather slow-growing to a height of about 9 ft., and is not particular as to soil and situation, though it is mostly seen clothing a wall. Knap Hill Scarlet is a salmon-red variety, 5–7 ft. tall, and Rowallane Seedling an intense and brilliant red, low-growing to 4 ft. Prune by cutting back new growth by about half to a convenient bud in the summer, and by removing the side shoots so that a short stub is left, two or three buds long, in winter. (See also Shrubs with attractive fruits page 33.)

Choisya The strong, sweet scent of the Mexican orange blossom, *Choisya ternata,* is intensified if the bush is planted in a warm spot, but even without this it still flowers prolifically, its white, yellow-stamened flowers etched against its glossy evergreen leaves in May, and spasmodically in the autumn too. It is quite hardy, although in the north of England it is better against a south-facing wall. Little pruning is required, except to remove straggling shoots and dead flowerheads to encourage a second, later crop. It will grow well in most soils, including chalky ones.

Coronilla This yellow-flowered shrub is a member of the Pea family and produces clusters of flowers, shaped like miniature sweet peas, abundantly in April, and spasmodically throughout the summer as well. *Coronilla glauca* is not truly hardy, and needs a warm, south-facing wall, with protection in winter; it reaches about 5 ft. outside but perhaps

(Top)
Camellia japonica donckelarii, with semi-double, dark red flowers marked with white, is a favourite variety of many gardeners

(Bottom)
Brilliant red flowers and low, spreading habit make *Chaenomeles speciosa* Rowallane Seedling a useful shrub for many gardens

(Top)

The graceful evergreen *Berberis stenophylla*, one of the best-known of all the barberries. It is specially useful as a hedging plant

(Bottom)

Cytisus scoparius sulphureus, often called the moonlight broom, is an excellent 'point' plant for a prominent position. All brooms need bright, sunny positions

double that in a greenhouse or its natural habitat, southern Europe. It will grow in most soils. Prune the tips of the shoots after flowering: this will encourage it to remain compact and bushy. It is evergreen.

Cytisus Also a member of the Pea family, *Cytisus scoparius*, the common yellow broom, and its named hybrids flower in May and reach a height of about 8 ft. Good varieties are: Diana, white and yellow; Donard Seedling, deep and light pink; Firefly, crimson and yellow, and *sulphureus*, deep cream. These hybrids are not very good on limy soils, and grow much better on only slightly limy or neutral ones. *C. kewensis* is a prostrate-growing hybrid covered in creamy flowers in spring, and suitable for the rock garden. In general, light, rather poor soils in sunny positions suit brooms best. Cut back immediately after flowering, removing old flowered shoots for two-thirds their length. It is essential to prune the upright-growing kinds in this way to keep them bushy and encourage flowering.

Forsythia A more profusely-flowering shrub it would be difficult to find – the bush is one mass of bright golden flowers in early spring – provided the birds leave the buds alone. They may attack the bush in February, but sometimes may start to 'disbud' in November of the previous year. Bird prevention sprays help, but most need to be renewed after rain or snow. Special rayon netting rather like spiders' webs may also prove effective. Prune only to thin out the growth every few years after flowering, removing the flowered shoots back to new growth; when grown against walls, prune every year. *Forsythia intermedia* Lynwood is one of the best, growing to 10 ft., but *F. ovata* is another good sort, flowering in very early spring, sometimes even February, and only growing to 4 or 5 ft. Its leaves change to a light golden-brown shade in autumn, and it will grow into a prettily shaped bush without pruning. All forsythias grow well in ordinary soils including limy ones, in full sun or partial shade.

Genista Late spring- and early summer-flowering, the genistas have bright yellow flowers very thickly produced all over the bush. There are dwarf kinds, suitable for the rock garden, only a few inches high; others of medium height, to 2 or 3 ft., and one or two, such as the Mount Etna broom, *Genista aethnensis,* to 12 ft.; *G. lydia* reaches 3 ft. and is covered in golden flowers in May. Pruning is not necessary. They like warm sunny positions with well-drained soils.

Peony The shrubby peonies are spectacularly lovely plants. The May-flowering *Paeonia suffruticosa* is an original species from which garden forms and hybrids have been obtained. It has large white flowers with petals apparently made of crinkled tissue paper, with a deep magenta blotch at the base and centred with golden stamens. The species itself is beautiful, and the garden forms and hybrids bred from it even lovelier. Elizabeth is an example of such a hybrid. *P. suffruticosa* grows to about 4 ft. high, and rather more in width. It is inclined to start into growth too early in the year, as soon as there is a mild spell, is cut back by subsequent colder weather and often never does really well as a result. It is best to put it into a sheltered position where the sun is unlikely to reach it until after midday during the winter and early spring, so as to avoid as far as possible alternation of cold and warmth while it is supposedly dormant. It flowers in May and needs a deep, fairly rich soil, and is therefore helped by feeding heavily with compost each spring.

Rhododendrons and azaleas Azaleas are included here as they are regarded by the botanists as being a section of the genus *Rhododendron*; in nurserymen's catalogues they may be listed under azaleas or rhododendrons. For those who are lucky enough to garden on acid soils, one or two of these

(Top)
Coronilla glauca needs the protection of a warm, south-facing wall and further protection in winter. It is well worth coddling

(Bottom)
The low-growing Genista lydia which flowers in May is a shrub of the highest quality. Sunshine and good drainage are essential requirements

shrubs are essential. Every colour can be found amongst them, and the low-growing Japanese, Ghent and *mollis* azalea hybrids are particularly lovely, flowering in April and May. Rhododendrons are somewhat taller, on the whole, although *Rhododendron fastigiatum* is a dwarf kind reaching 2–3 ft., and flowering in April and May. These shrubs are not deep-rooting; nevertheless they must have good drainage and a soil containing leafmould. Failing this they should be heavily mulched with leafmould or peat each year in spring. Light shade, or filtered sunlight under trees suits them, and little pruning is required except to remove the dead flowerheads as soon as they have finished blooming, since otherwise the bushes exhaust their strength in producing seed. There are evergreen and deciduous kinds of azaleas; rhododendrons are all evergreen. *R. praecox* flowers in March, or even a little earlier, and will reach 3–5 ft.; it is semi-evergreen.

(Top left)
Cytisus kewensis – a prostrate-growing shrub which is well suited for the rock garden. The flowers are cream coloured

(Bottom left)
Smaller growing than other forsythias, the pale yellow *Forsythia ovata* flowers in very early spring, sometimes even in February

(Top right)
Arching sprays of white flowers in spring make *Spiraea arguta* a handsome shrub for a prominent position in the shrub border

Spiraea There are two types of spiraea, those that flower in spring and have white sprays of flowers and those that bloom in late summer, having pink, red or white flowers. The spring-flowering kinds include *Spiraea arguta*, to 7 ft., with arching sprays of flowers, often known as Bridal Wreath; *S. vanhouttei*, to 8 ft., and *S. thunbergii*, 3–5 ft. All these should be pruned immediately after flowering. They are easily-grown shrubs, more than re-paying the occasional feed or mulch.

Syringa Much better known as lilac, this is available today in very many lovely varieties, single and double flowered. As it is 10–15 ft. high when fully grown and takes up rather a lot of room it is well to remember that once it has flowered, it contributes little to the overall effect of a garden; indeed in winter, without leaves, it has rather an ungainly shape. Good double varieties are: Katherine Havemeyer, purple, fading to lilac; Mme Lemoine, white; Mrs Edward Harding, red shading to pink,

(Top left)
The pink-flowered **Tamarix tetranda**, a shrub for a sunny position. It is May flowering

(Top right)
The white, double-flowered **Syringa** Mme Lemoine has been a favourite of gardeners for very many years

(Bottom right)
A striking single-flowered syringa is the purple Prodige variety

(Top)
For a gay display the deciduous Ghent azaleas are unsurpassed - but, like all other azaleas and rhododendrons, a lime-free soil is a necessity

(Bottom)
The deciduous, May-flowering *Spiraea van-houttei* is a hybrid which flowers in May and reaches a height of 6 ft. or so

and President Grevy, bluish-lilac. Good singles are: Clarke's Giant, lilac-blue; Primrose, yellow; Prodige, deep purple; and Souvenir de Louis Spath, dark red. These hybrids all require good soil preparation before planting. Prune after flowering to remove old flowered shoots and weak ones. Feed with sulphate of potash, about a handful to each plant, at the same time.

Tamarix *Tamarix tetranda* is very like *T. pentandra*, described on page 21, but produces much lighter and more delicate pink flowers, very much earlier in the year, in May. It is pruned immediately after the flowers have finished, cutting out the shoots which have flowered. The tamarisks will grow in most soils and like a sunny position.

Weigela A genus of shrubs (sometimes known as Diervilla) not often seen, but perfectly easy to grow given a moderately rich soil. They are most attractive, with their arching shoots covered in funnel-shaped flowers in late spring. *Weigela florida* is rose, flowering in May – it reaches 6–8 ft. *W. middendorffiana*, 2–4 ft., has yellow flowers, spotted orange, in spring. *W. praecox* flowers in April – its rose flowers have a yellow throat. Prune immediately after flowering.

SUMMER-FLOWERING SHRUBS

Abutilon These are rather tender shrubs from South America, but so attractive that it is worth trying one against a sheltered south wall in the south or west of England. Their flowers are bell-shaped, produced in June and July; Ashford Red is a particularly pretty variety with large, red flowers throughout the summer. It grows to about 8 ft. *Abutilon megapotamicum* has smaller, yellow bells, with a red calyx, to the same height, and *variegatum* is a variation of this with attractively yellow-mottled leaves. *A. vitifolium* has lilac-coloured flowers and large, soft, vine-like leaves; it grows to a height of about 15 ft. These species enjoy sun and well-drained soil. Prune in spring, cutting back to new growth but do not remove all the old flowering wood each time.

Buddleia Fat, soft spikes of purple, lavender, red, plum, white and near-black are evidence of the buddleia's wide colour range. Ridiculously easy to grow on almost any soil, although they prefer those that are reasonably well drained. They repay pruning a hundred-fold with their prolific flowering in late summer and autumn. Cut back in spring those shoots that have flowered the previous summer, not too hard in cold districts, otherwise they are likely to die. Chalky soils suit them, and butterflies love them. *Buddleia alternifolia* can be trained as a standard, to produce a waterfall of lilac-coloured flowers from mid-summer to autumn, and *B. fallowiana* is an extremely pretty species, with blue flowers produced in August and silvery-grey leaves. Height of all types varies between 8–12 ft. Some good varieties of *B. davidii* are: Black Knight, black-purple; Fortune, lilac; Royal Red, deep plum; and White Cloud.

Convolvulus An extremely attractive shrub, *Convolvulus cneorum* produces its yellow-centred, funnel-shaped, white flowers in summer on bushes 2–3 ft. high; the leaves are 'evergrey'. It likes very well-drained soil and a hot, sunny position, and it needs protection in winter, but it is worth a little trouble.

Cytisus The species *Cytisus battandieri*, blooming in June, has quite different flowers to those species described under cytisus on page 10; they grow in fat, yellow, curving, spike-like groups, with an intense scent of pineapples, and with silky, greyish-green leaves. This shrub is quite outstanding and reaches 10–12 ft. See page 10 for pruning.

Deutzia Easily-grown shrubs to about 6 ft., and doing well on chalk soils, deutzias are heavy flowerers, producing single and double, rather fringe-like, mainly white flowers, from May to July. Their delicate bell-shaped

(Top)
The beautiful *Abutilon megapotamicum* is a possibility outdoors for those fortunate gardeners who live in mild counties, and have a sunny wall against which to grow it

(Bottom)
Buddleia davidii White Cloud, a variety which can be effectively used as a specimen plant or as contrast for strongly-coloured shrubs

blooms make a pleasing contrast with the other heavier, more voluptuous summer flowers, such as hydrangeas and peonies. *Deutzia longifolia*, 4–6 ft., rose-pink single flowers; *D. scabra*, 8 ft., white or pinkish, single flowers; *D. s. candidissima*, pure white, double flowers and *D. s. plena*, white flowers stained with rose-purple outside.

Escallonia A graceful family of shrubs, with curving sprays of rose, pink or white flowers, not very large but making up for their small size by their profusion; they are produced from June onwards. Escallonias are evergreen and reach a height which varies between 8 and 12 ft., and make good seaside hedges. They will grow in any reasonably good soil and like sunny places. Particularly good forms are: *Escallonia macrantha*, with rosy-crimson flowers; Pink Pearl, rose-pink; Slieve Donard, pink; Donard Seedling with pink buds, changing to white as the flowers open; and *E. langleyensis*, with rose-red flowers; the last-named reaches about 6 ft. Pruning in the spring to remove last year's flowering shoots is necessary to keep them well covered each year.

Euphorbia The spurges contain some plants of considerable interest, in particular *Euphorbia characias* and *E. wulfenii*, both of which are sub-shrubs (in other words the tips of the shoots are cut back each winter). *E. characias* has enormous heads of yellowish-green flowers, with red 'eyes' during summer, backed by bluish-green narrow leaves. *E. wulfenii* has much yellower, looser heads and flowers earlier in May; the individual flowers are more of a bell shape and the leaves are evergreen. Both are hardy unless the winter is very cold, and both need little pruning. Cut out the oldest shoots so that new ones will grow. It reaches 4 ft.

Fremontia As is suggested by the name, *Fremontia californica* is a native of California, where it may reach 30 ft. in that State's somewhat mellower climate. In the south-west and sheltered south of England, grown against a west- or south-facing wall, it is more likely to grow to about 15 ft., and will produce large, golden flowers, round and saucer-shaped, $2\frac{1}{2}$ in. across, the whole summer through, starting in May. It does not like its feet in wet soil so make sure that the large quantities of water it requires can travel through the soil easily.

Fuchsia The little red and purple flowers of *Fuchsia gracilis*, exactly like ballet dancers in red and purple skirts, are produced on arching sprays in summer, from June to September. This fuchsia makes 6-ft. high hedges in the West, but in the rest of the country makes rounded bushes about 4 ft. high. The plant should be protected with a thick mulch several inches deep, during the winter, and in spring cut back almost to ground level. *F. magellanica versicolor* has cream-variegated foliage, tinted with pink, and *F. m. discolor* has larger flowers, with lighter-coloured purple petals. Double hybrid fuchsias can also be grown out of doors, but the risk of losing them in a hard winter is much greater, and they will need considerably more protection, perhaps even lifting and putting in the greenhouse. They like well-drained but not dry soils and a sunny or partially-shaded position.

Hydrangea The great pink, red, purple and blue mop heads of the Hortensia type of hydrangea (varieties of *H. macrophylla* var. *hortensia*) need no description. They are versatile shrubs that will grow in sun or semi-shade, and are equally at home as specimens, or as hedges, growing in seaside districts, in woodlands, or as pot plants. Good varieties are: Générale Vicomtesse de Vibraye, pink, but light blue on acid soils; Maréchal Foch, deep rose, purple-blue on acid soils; Mme E. Mouillière, white; Ami Pasquier, crimson; Westfalen, deep red or

(Top)
If a warm, sheltered south-facing wall is available, the red-flowered *Abutilon* Ashford Red is a highly-decorative shrub to consider growing

(Bottom)
The showy white flowerheads of tall-flowering *Hydrangea paniculata* are borne at a useful time – late summer

(Top)
The Hortensia hydrangea variety Westfalen, which has deep red or mauve flowers

(Bottom)
The tree lupin, *Lupinus arboreus*, which can be easily raised from seed

(Top)
As if it needed further attributes, *Cytisus battandieri* adds a pineapple fragrance to its other charms

(Bottom)
The June to July-flowering *Deutzia scabra*, a member of an easily-grown genus which does well on chalky soils

mauve flowers. Blueing hydrangeas on very limy soils is not practicable; on slightly limy soils the use of aluminium sulphate at 4 oz. per gallon of water may be tried in February – more than one application may be needed at monthly intervals. Little pruning is required except to thin out young shoots as they emerge in spring if they are too crowded. Leave the dead flowerheads on the plant through the winter to protect the new buds. In addition to the Hortensia hydrangeas, there are others which are equally attractive. For instance, *H. sargentiana*, 6–10 ft., has thickly-haired stems and large hairy leaves; its flowers are bluish-white. It prefers light shade and shelter from cold winds. *H. macrophylla mariesii* produces hydrangea flowers known as 'lace-caps' which have flat, rather than round, heads of flowers. *H. m. mariesii* is pink; Blue Wave is a good, late-summer-flowering variety and Lanarth White one of the best white ones. *H. paniculata* has white pyramidal heads of flowers in late summer, these later turning pink – the plant reaches about 10 ft. Prune this species hard in spring, cutting the shoots back to a few inches and reducing their number considerably, and feed generously at the same time to obtain flowerheads which can be as much as 1–1½ ft. across.

Hypericum Very attractive shrubs, varying from the ground-cover type to those about 6 ft. high; their flowers are golden yellow, saucer shaped, with prominent brush-like stamens, and are produced in profusion in sun or shade. *Hypericum patulum* Hidcote flowers July–August and reaches 6–7 ft., and is covered with golden flowers. *H. calycinum* flowers in mid-summer and goes on till the end of August. This shrub makes excellent ground cover and has a liking for chalky soils. It is evergreen and has the typical yellow flowers with prominent stamens. *H. moserianum* has similar flowers 2½ in. across but with pink stamens. Little pruning is required.

(Top)
For those who prefer shades of pink, *Escallonia langleyensis* is a natural choice for colour from June onwards

(Bottom)
A shrub for a south-facing wall in various gardens is *Fremontia californica*, which flowers freely during the summer

(Top)
Hypericum Hidcote, a large-flowered variety which could be an asset to any garden during its flowering season, from mid-summer to August

(Bottom)
Like the rhododendrons, *Kalmia latifolia* is only for lime-free soils. It needs a lightly-shaded site and has flowers of fine substance and beauty

(Top)
Philadelphus Belle Etoile, which has purple centres to its white flowers, has a particularly pleasing scent

(Bottom)
Philadelphus Virginal, a double-flowered variety of fine quality

Kalmia The unusual shape of the kalmia's pink flowers make it doubly attractive and they will be plentifully produced when grown in acid soil with plenty of compost, and a lightly shaded site. It is June flowering. *Kalmia latifolia* reaches about 8 ft. and *K. l. myrtifolia* is a low-growing form. It is an evergreen.

Lavandula The secret of growing good lavender is to clip it back so that it does not become straggly, doing this with a pair of shears each spring. Its purple-blue spikes of flowers are enhanced by the greyish-silvery, needle-like leaves and, as it is a native of the Mediterranean region, a warm spot with a well-drained light soil, will produce the best plants, which will grow to about 4 ft. high. Hedges or specimen plants are equally pleasing; *Lavandula spica* is the common sort. There is a shorter variety called Hidcote with deep, purple-blue flowers but it does not have such a strong scent.

Lupin The tree lupin, *Lupinus arboreus*, is easily grown from seed and grows fast, reaching 3 or 4 ft. in one season with a markedly woody stem. It eventually grows to about 8 ft. Flowers are yellow or white, and freely produced; the tree is short lived, making it a good shrub to fill in a temporary gap. It will grow in poor, sandy soils.

Philadelphus This is mock orange blossom, flowering in June or July and growing to about 10–12 ft. Its white, 4-petalled flowers with golden stamens, sweet scent and its ease of cultivation make it a popular shrub with gardeners. Shoots should be removed after flowering, cutting them back to the strong new shoots which already will be growing fast. Belle Etoile is a variety with purple marking at the centre of the flowers and a particularly pleasing scent. Virginal is a double white-flowered variety, and Manteau d'Hermine has creamy-yellow flowers, also double. Like the others it is fragrant, but grows only to a height of about 4 ft. All grow easily in poor soil.

Phlomis The Jerusalem sage, *Phlomis fruticosa,* has heads of yellow, hooded flowers, backed by 'evergrey' felted leaves, and makes a rounded low-growing plant about 3 ft. high. It is hardy except in really cold areas and is particularly good in a sunny spot as it likes warmth and good drainage. Do not prune.

Spiraea *Spiraea menziesii triumphans* has purplish-pink spikes of flowers about 8 in. long, in August, on bushes 3–5 ft. high. *S. douglasii* is 4–6 ft., flowering earlier in June and July, with purplish-rose spikes 4–8 in. long. See also page 13.

Tamarix Sugar-pink feathery, rather frond-like flowerheads are the tamarisk's main attraction. From a distance the plant looks rather like a gigantic pink feather duster, eventually reaching about 12–15 ft. high. *Tamarix pentandra* comes from the south-west Mediterranean region, and flowers in July–August; the leaves are small, needle-like and insignificant. It grows well at seasides defying the coastal gales and salt spray. Prune it in April, cutting back the shoots that flowered the previous year quite severely – this will make it flower more abundantly (see page 14 for spring-flowering species).

Viburnum A diverse, easily-grown genus which has plants flowering right through the year, and also has some most attractive berries and foliage. Summer-flowering species include the guelder rose, *Viburnum opulus sterile*, deciduous, 10–12 ft., which has white, snowball-like clusters of flowers in June. *V. tomentosum mariesii* is a very handsome shrub, flowering in June and reaching 6–10 ft. and more in favourable situations. The flowers are produced along the length of the horizontal branches, giving a pagoda-like effect; red berries turning black follow the flowers. Routine pruning for viburnums is not required, only tidying up (see also under winter flowers page 27 and berries page 36).

(Below)
***Tamarix pentandra*, with pink flowers, is specially suitable for seaside planting**

shrubs for autumn and winter

The late summer and early autumn are times of the year when the garden can begin to look a little tired and dusty, when shrubs tend to produce berries rather than flowers, and when foliage changes to its autumn colouring.

However, there are in fact plenty of shrubs whose best display only now begins. These will provide flower colour until the first frosts. Following these are the shrubs which only flower in winter and, more often than not, are very sweetly scented.

AUTUMN-FLOWERING SHRUBS

Calluna The native heather, *Calluna vulgaris*, is found on Scottish and English moors and hills. It begins flowering in August and continues through until November. Much hybridising and collecting of specially good wild forms have occurred, and there are many most attractive varieties in all shades of pink, red, purple and rose, and many others which are strikingly attractive for their foliage. They must have acid soils, preferably containing peat – leafmould will make a good substitute provided it is not from trees growing on chalky soil – and they should be trimmed over in April. *C. v.* H. E. Beale is a variety of *Calluna vulgaris* with long spikes of deep pink, double flowers thickly clustered on the stem; *C. v. searlei* has long white flower spikes and bright green foliage; *C. v.* Gold Haze really does have bright, golden foliage all year round;

C. v. Goldsworth Crimson is deep red, flowering very late.

Caryopteris These are late-flowering shrubs, not starting until September. Sometimes known as the blue spiraea, they have greyish-green leaves and extremely attractive flowers in varying shades of blue. *Caryopteris clandonensis* reaches about 4 ft., but can be kept shorter than this by careful pruning. Heavenly Blue is similar but a little taller and a darker blue. Caryopteris do best in sun and well-drained soils and should be pruned in spring, cutting back almost to ground level.

Ceanothus There are not many shrubs with blue flowers, but ceanothus is one of them. Flowering time varies from spring to autumn according to species and variety, and Gloire de Versailles, a particularly good variety, has light blue flowers in late summer and autumn. Autumnal Blue, evergreen, has dark blue, rather stout flower spikes. Henri Defosse also has deep blue flowers, but with a hint of purple in them. If evergreen, ceanothus are not completely hardy, and all do best if grown against walls. They can be trained easily to any shape, and time of pruning varies according to the rules given on page 58.

(Right)
Hibiscus syriacus Woodbridge. The tree holly-hocks, as the hibiscuses are called, need a sunny position and well-drained soil. They flower from August into late September

(Top)
The aptly-named winter sweet, *Chimonanthus praecox*, produces its distinctive flowers in December and January

(Bottom)
A close mat of the *Erica carnea* varieties Springwood, white, and Springwood Pink, is a splendid way of bringing colour to the winter garden

Hebe These little shrubs, once called veronicas, produce delightful spikes of blue, purple, red, pink or white flowers from late summer till October. They are evergreen, growing to 3 or 4 ft. high and make a most useful addition to the autumn display. *Hebe* Carl Teschner is purple, 1 ft.; La Seduisante, brilliant reddish-plum-coloured spikes of flowers; *H. lindsayi* has short, bright pink flower spikes, and Simon Delaux, deep red ones. *H. brachysiphon* grows somewhat taller than the average, to about 5 ft., and has white flowers in June. *H. andersonii variegata* has blue-violet spikes in late summer and autumn, and white variegated leaves; it reaches about 4 ft. Prune in spring to keep the plants' shape attractive and remove straggling shoots.

Hibiscus A shrub with a name so evocative of the South Seas seems unlikely to make much of a display in chilly English gardens but the varieties of the shrubby *Hibiscus syriacus* produce a surprising profusion of flowers in pink, rosy-red, purple, blue and white. They are the authentic hibiscus shape, with crinkled crepe-paper petals. Give them a sunny position and good, well-drained soil and do not prune except to tidy the outline. Hamabo is pink with a deep red centre; Blue Bird is blue with a red centre; *elegantissimus* is a double white with a crimson centre, and Woodbridge is a deep pink with a crimson centre. Coeleste is a single variety with deep blue flowers. They reach a height of about 8 ft.

Indigofera A member of the *Leguminosae*, the Pea family, indigoferas have feathery leaves and a graceful habit of growth. They flower throughout the summer and autumn. *Indigofera potaninii* has pink flowers, rather than the usual purple, as has *I. gerardiana*. Both reach 5 ft. or a little more, require little pruning and are not particular as to soil.

Lespedeza Bright, rose-purple, pea-like flowers in graceful hanging clusters late in the season characterise this shrub. *Lespedeza* *thunbergii* is one of the best species, and its large rosy-purple flowers are set off by the trifoliate formation of the leaves. Prune lightly in spring. This shrub may be spoilt if the weather turns cold early in the autumn, but it flowers so heavily that it is worth trying for that time of the year when shrubs, and indeed most plants, are ceasing, or have already ceased, to flower. It is not particular as to soil, but a cold windy situation should be avoided to get the best from it. It grows to 5 ft.

WINTER-FLOWERING SHRUBS

Chimonanthus The winter sweet, *Chimonanthus praecox*, which grows to 9 ft., has yellow and red, spiky flowers, which unexpectedly unfold from round buds. The scent of these flowers is extremely strong and most attractive to come across suddenly on a cold winter's day. The leaves follow the flowers. It is not easy to grow and may take two or three years to establish itself, and although hardy it appreciates the protection of a wall or other sheltered positions and a good well-drained soil; in severe winters it may be killed. Little pruning is required.

Erica The heaths flower from January to April in the species *Erica carnea*, which also has the advantage that it will grow on limy soils, as well as acid ones, unlike the callunas mentioned on page 22. Good varieties are: Springwood, white; Springwood Pink; *vivellii*, deep red and rather low growing, with dark green leaves, browny-red in winter, later than the type; Ruby Glow, deep rose with brownish-green foliage, and Winter Beauty which starts really early in December and has bright pink flowers. Trim over in the spring after flowering to remove flowered shoots. Soil should be well drained and light. (The remainder of the ericas mostly flower in the summer and autumn.)

Garrya The only species is *Garrya elliptica*, an evergreen shrub from California which has

(Top)
The catkins of *Garrya elliptica* can be an eye-catching spectacle in January and February on a well-developed specimen. Usually grown against walls, they can be grown as free-standing shrubs in milder districts

(Bottom)
The upright-growing, deciduous *Viburnum fragrans*, which flowers from early winter to spring in reasonable weather

(Top)
Gold is a colour not usually associated with heathers by most gardeners. *Calluna vulgaris* Gold Haze makes its own distinctive contribution with its cheery colouring

(Bottom)
***Caryopteris clandonensis*, sometimes known as the blue spiraea, is valuable for its late flowering in September and October**

the merit of growing well in any aspect, though in colder gardens it will grow better on a warm wall, and help to clothe it very attractively. It makes a plant about 12 ft. high, and during January and February, under favourable conditions, produces catkin-like pendulous flowers, silvery-green in colour, about 9–12 in. in length. The female, rarely seen, produces almost as effective long, pendulous clusters of black fruits. It will grow in any good well-drained soil and likes a sunny sheltered position. Pruning is not required for this shrub.

Hamamelis The Chinese and Japanese witch-hazels start to uncurl their spider-like yellow flowers in December and continue right through January even when there is snow on the ground. There may still be the occasional flowers left in spring when the leaves start to appear, and they have the added merit that in autumn the leaves turn pleasing shades of yellow, red and brown. Slow-growing to 15 ft., they require little pruning except to improve the shape, or to make them rather bushier, by cutting back the tips to encourage side shoots to sprout. *Hamamelis mollis* is the best sort; others with orange or paler yellow petals are not so easy to grow. All will thrive in good, slightly moist soils in open or partly-shaded places.

Jasminum It is surprising that the heavily-scented jasmine or jessamine, *Jasminum officinale*, from Persia and Kashmir, should have a near relation which not only flowers in this country but does it during the coldest time of the year. *Jasminum nudiflorum* opens its bright yellow, primrose-like flowers from mid-November onwards until the end of January or through February, even in snow. It succeeds and looks best against a wall, as it requires some support for its rather trailing habit, and grows in almost any soil to 15 ft. Prune after flowering to remove shoots that have flowered and tie the rest in place.

Mahonia These shrubs are evergreen, with glossy, prickly leaves rather like holly, and sprays of lemon-yellow, round flowers growing from a central point. In the species *Mahonia japonica*, 5–7 ft., the flowers have a lily-of-the-valley perfume, and are followed by dark blue berries. *M. aquifolium* is much lower growing, to only 3 ft. in some places, but has the typical yellow flowers in erect spikes, followed by purple berries. Also evergreen, the leaves turn reddish in winter. They will grow in any reasonably good soil. Pruning is not required except to keep a good shape.

Viburnum Two viburnums flower in winter: *Viburnum tinus*, or laurustinus, and *V. fragrans*. The former makes a nicely-shaped round shrub, reaching about 9 or 10 ft., evergreen, with clusters of flowers, pink in the bud and opening to white, all through the winter. Pruning is not required. *V. fragrans* is deciduous and makes more of a tree-like shape, rather upright. Its pink flowers start to appear in early winter and go on until spring. Their fragrance is very strong. Little pruning is required except to remove awkwardly placed or weak shoots. Both can add colour and cheer to the garden scene at a time when it is more than welcome.

(Bottom left)
The Chinese witch-hazel, *Hamamelis mollis*, one of the most welcome of all winter-flowering shrubs. It will grow slowly to a height of 15 ft.

(Top right)
Mahonia aquifolium, an easily-pleased winter-flowering shrub which makes a good ground-cover plant

(Bottom right)
The flowers of *Mahonia aquifolium* are followed by purple berries of considerable decorative value. The leaves also take on reddish tints later in the year

shrubs with special qualities

As has been mentioned, many shrubs are grown for other qualities as well as flowers. The most important of such qualities are foliage, climbing habit and attractive fruits; and they are so grouped in this chapter. Of course, many shrubs have more than one useful quality, so at the end of each section there is a list referring to shrubs described elsewhere in the book.

SHRUBS WITH GOOD FOLIAGE

One of the most exciting aspects of modern gardening is the increasing realisation that it is possible to 'paint' just as attractive pictures using plants whose leaves are their main attraction as it is using plants whose flowers are their most outstanding beauty. The architectural value of leaves can be one of their best qualities and this is used to striking effect by some gardeners, who combine shrubs, herbaceous plants, grasses, conifers and trees.

The colours of leaves are astonishingly varied. The greens alone contain an extremely subtle range of shades, very nearly impossible to reproduce in a painting, but besides these, leaf colours may be purple, red, yellow, blue, white, silver, grey and orange – in fact nearly every colour imaginable, exactly as they occur in flowers. True, colours tend to be simple, i.e. red, orange or blue, with little variation in tone, whereas in flowers the range in each colour is as great as the range of greens in leaves, but nevertheless the colours are there, and only need looking for; they are certainly not restricted to green as one usually imagines.

Conifers The variation in the colour of the foliage of conifers has to be seen to be believed. *Thuya orientalis* has golden tips to its fan-shaped sprays of 'leaves' giving it an all-over sunny effect; *Taxus baccata fastigiata aurea*, the upright-growing variety of the golden yew, gives a much more golden effect rather than a yellow-green appearance. One or two conifers in the garden can add immeasurably to the setting for the flowering plants and are most attractive in the bleak winter months.

Corylus The Hazel Nut family has a member with striking dark purple leaves – this is *Corylus maxima atropurpurea*. It reaches a height of 12–15 ft. and makes a handsome specimen. It is deciduous.

Cotinus A shrub with the tongue-twisting name of *Cotinus coggygria foliis purpureis* has deciduous purple leaves, becoming reddish towards autumn; they make a good foil for silvery-leaved herbaceous plants, or other shrubs. *C. c. atropurpureus,* also deciduous, is another shrub known as the smoke bush because of its feathery inflorescences – pinkish in colour – which, from a distance, resemble clouds of smoke all over the bush. The leaves turn brilliant yellow in the autumn.

Elaeagnus These are handsome evergreen shrubs, with oval pointed-tipped leaves. They make good barriers against the wind. *Elaeagnus pungens variegata* has narrow, light yellow leaf margins, and *E. p. maculata* has yellow spots and patches on the leaves. *E. pungens dicksonii* has deep golden variegation and is rather slow growing. *E. macrophylla* has leaves which are silvered on both sides, the upper side turning bright green as the summer goes on. It has also yellow, rather insignificant flowers in November, which make up for their smallness by their fragrance. Height of all these is about 6 ft. The deciduous-leaved species are not so useful since, besides losing their leaves in winter, the flowers are very small and rather pale, although scented.

Euonymus The common name for *Euonymus europaeus* is the spindle tree, and its orange and rose-pink fruits are well known. However, there are some evergreen species which have most attractive foliage and help to improve the look of the garden in winter, as well as giving it a framework in the summer for the brighter and more varied colours of herbaceous plants. *E. fortunei* Silver Queen is one of these, a shrub to be used either as ground cover or for growing on walls. The leaves are variegated with white and are most effective in dark places. *E. japonicus aureopictus* has dark green shiny leaves with a central golden yellow blotch and makes a good hedge or an attractive individual specimen. *E. j. macrophyllus albus* has a leaf with a wide margin, very conspicuous, and *E. j. ovatus aureus* has leaves with large patches of yellow and a generally yellow tone. No pruning is needed except to keep the shape, or to remove the occasional reverted, plain green-leaved shoot.

Fothergilla For autumn colouring, on the right soils *Fothergilla major* would be hard to beat as a choice of shrub with its orange, brown and yellow leaves. This is a shrub for soils with an acid reaction, preferably containing sand and plenty of peat or leafmould.

Height is about 8 ft.; it has the additional merit of rather fluffy yellow and pinkish-white 'flowers' in spring. The flowers are in fact the stamens, the petals being so reduced as to be insignificant. Prune after flowering.

Hedera The common or garden ivy, *Hedera helix*, is in itself attractive with its evergreen three-lobed leaves, but there are now some even more interesting ones to be grown. For instance *H. colchica dentata variegata* makes a striking covering for a wall or fence or for scrambling over dead trees, pillars and other supports. It can even be allowed to trail along the ground. Its pale yellow variegation on the leaves stands out well in shaded situations or makes a most attractive addition to the colour of a mixed border. *H. helix purpurea* is exactly like the common ivy, but in winter the leaves turn a deep purple. *H. h. marginata* has leaves with creamy-white margins; these turn pink in winter. Cut back only to keep under control.

Salvia A low-growing shrub, *Salvia officinalis purpurascens* has the typical greyish-green leaves of sage, but they are blotched and marked with creamy-white and purple, and have an all-over purplish tinge. This sage is definitely for those who like something different. Height is 2½–3 ft., and it needs dividing and replanting every few years to prevent it becoming thin and straggly. A sunny position suits it best, with protection in cold areas.

Senecio These are low-growing shrubs generally from New Zealand, mostly with attractive silvery foliage, particularly in the variety *Senecio cineraria* White Diamond. This has almost white leaves, deeply cut and serrated at the margins, providing a perfect contrast to bedding plants or any brilliantly-coloured herbaceous plants. *S. laxifolius* has greyish-green leaves, not cut and serrated, but oval-shaped with entire margins. It has yellow daisy-like flowers in June–July on a bush to about 3 ft. high. Neither of these is

deciduous and both do best in sun and rather dry soil; White Diamond in particular should be protected from winter damp and cold. Prune *S. laxifolius* in spring.

Vitis For really brilliant colouring of the leaves in autumn, *Vitis coignetiae* is hard to beat. This member of the ornamental vine family has large, deeply-veined and indented, lobed leaves, as much as 9 or 10 in. across and is invaluable for covering walls or fences. *Parthenocissus henryana* is another delightful vine, with silver and pink variegation on the leaves. It is self-clinging and is best coloured if grown in light shade. The leaves become red all over in the autumn and fall later. All will grow in any reasonable soil and in shade or sun although they prefer the latter.

For other shrubs with good foliage, see also the following, which have either evergreen leaves or coloured leaves in autumn, under flowering shrubs: berberis (p. 8), ceanothus (p. 9 and 22), choisya (p. 9), escallonia (p. 16), garrya (p. 25), hamamelis (p. 26), hebe (p. 24), hypericum (p. 18), kalmia (p. 20), mahonia (p. 27), phlomis (p. 21), rhododendron (p. 11), viburnum (p. 21 and 27).

CLIMBING SHRUBS GROWN FOR FLOWERS

Clematis The modern forms of clematis, related to our native plant old man's beard, *Clematis vitalba*, are amongst some of the most attractive climbing plants available. They do well on chalky soils, and, provided they do not die with that mysterious disease known as clematis wilt, have long and vigorous lives. They require well-drained soil and should have their roots shaded, though their top growth can be in sun. Mulching every spring with some form of bulky organic matter is advisable.

Clematis wilt is thought to be a fungus disease, which enters through an injury low down on the stem, often when the plant is

(Top)
The autumn colour of *Fothergilla major*, a shrub for acid soils

(Bottom)
Hedera colchica dentata variegata - a striking covering for a wall or fence

(Top)
The evergreen *Senecio laxifolius*, gay in mid-summer with its daisy-like flowers, is also a splendid shrub to provide a foil for other decorative plants

(Bottom)
Vitis coignetiae, invaluable as a wall cover providing colourful autumn tints

(Top)
For providing contrast in the border, *Senecio cineraria* White Diamond, 2¼ ft. tall and up to 4 ft. wide, is in a class of its own

(Bottom)
A handsome spring-flowering shrub for a warm corner is the evergreen, white-flowered clematis, variety Apple Blossom

young, and the stem has become twisted or kinked, either while planting or later because of a too-weak support while the plant is getting established. The only remedy is to cut below the wilted portion at once to prevent the disease spreading downwards, and hope that fresh growth will then start below the cut.

For flowering in spring, *Clematis armandii* Snowdrift and Apple Blossom, white and pink respectively, will produce drifts of blossom; they are particularly good against a south- or west-facing wall, protected from cold winds. For summer-flowering the hybrids are excellent; some varieties are: Comtesse de Bouchaud, pale rosy-pink, June to October; Ernest Markham, deep red, July to September; Etoile Violette, deep purple flowers in July for about a month; *C. jackmanii*, violet-purple, July to August; Lasurstern, purplish-blue, particularly large flowers, May to June and September; Marie Boisselot, white with prominent golden stamens, June to August; Nelly Moser, mauve-pink with a central reddish-pink bar on each petal, May to June and September and Perle d'Azur, light blue with a very faint bar, July. For late-flowering, *C. orientalis* has yellow flowers, from August to October, and *C. tangutica* Gravetye has yellow lantern-like flowers from August to October, followed by the typical old man's beard seedheads.

Pruning varies according to the type of clematis. The *patens* group, to which Lasurstern and Nelly Moser belong, bloom early in summer and should be pruned lightly after flowering, cutting back tips of shoots to strong buds, immediately below dead flowers; often they will then bloom again later. The *lanuginosa*, *jackmanii* and *viticella* groups, to which the remainder of the hybrid varieties mentioned belong, should be cut back hard in February or early March to within 12–18 in. from the ground; this type of pruning will

produce flowers in summer and autumn. *C. armandii* is pruned as soon as the flowers die, mainly to keep it in bounds; *C. orientalis* and *C. tangutica* in spring, cutting back last year's growth fairly hard.

Lonicera Honeysuckles are native plants and so present no difficulties in growing as they thrive in almost any soil. *Lonicera periclymenum* is the British species and the varieties *belgica* and *serotina* are improved forms of it, flowering in May–June and July–October respectively; both are very sweet smelling, with creamy-yellow flowers, pink on the outside, but rather shrubbier in habit of growth than the type.

Passiflora The passion flower, *Passiflora caerulea*, is a tender plant and will generally grow really well only in good soil on a south- or west-facing wall in the west country. However, it has been known to survive winters out of doors much farther east, admittedly mild ones, and with protection in the form of a heavy mulch is worth trying out of doors in sheltered situations. Plants have been known to be hardy in London. The remarkable flowers, with their greenish-white sepals and dark blue centres make an exotic-looking flower, lavishly produced all along the twining stems, from July to the end of September and even into October. Prune in April, shortening the small side shoots.

Polygonum The Russian vine, or 'mile-a-minute' vine's chief merit is covering ugly walls, fences, sides of sheds and garages very quickly. Its rate of growth is phenomenal, and from July to September it produces feathery plume-like clusters of flowers, white to cream in colour, all over it. *Polygonum baldschuanicum* only requires pruning to keep it in bounds.

Solanum A member of the same family as the potato, *Solanum crispum* can climb as high as 25 ft. in warm situations. It should be grown against a south- or west-facing wall,

except in the south, and requires protection from frost. The lilac-purple flowers with yellow centres are freely produced from June to September and fairly hard pruning should be done in spring, to encourage the production of new growth, and to keep the shrub's growth under control.

Wisteria The pale violet flowers of this twining plant from the Far East are produced in May and early June. Wisteria can be difficult to establish, but once it is flourishing, its long, hanging plumes of flowers surrounded by the pinnate leaves would be difficult to improve on, and with the right pruning are produced in abundance; they quite often appear again later in the year or at intervals throughout the season. *Wisteria sinensis* is the usual species; *W. floribunda macrobotrys* is a variety with particularly long racemes of flowers, to as much as $2\frac{1}{2}$ ft. in favourable situations. A white variety can be obtained, *W. f. alba*, attractive growing against a red brick wall, or with a dark background to set it off; its plumes of flowers are not so long. Wisterias like sunny positions and prefer a fairly rich soil though they will grow in almost any soil. Prune wisterias in summer to cut back the new shoots to within four or five buds, or leaves, and then prune again in winter shortening these shoots even further. Tie in the new growths against the support and allow the leading shoot to go on until the required height is reached.

For other climbing shrubs, see also hedera (p. 29) and vitis (p. 30), under foliage. *Jasminum nudiflorum* (p. 26) under winter-flowering shrubs is also used as a climber.

SHRUBS WITH ATTRACTIVE FRUITS

Chaenomeles The golden quinces of japonica are very handsome, and are most likely to be seen on the species *Chaenomeles japonica alpina* or *C. j.* Boule de Feu. *C. cathayensis* produces large oval-shaped fruits. Any of these can be used for making quince jam or jelly (see also page 9).

Colutea The yellow pea flowers of *Colutea arborescens* are followed by bladder-like, translucent fruits. These are hollow with a small seed inside, and they will last through most of the winter.

Cotoneaster The cotoneasters, as well as being very good spring-flowering shrubs, also have berries in the autumn in brilliant reds, oranges and yellows. Each shoot will be a mass of berries and they are really most effective through the autumn and the early part of the winter; some even go on right through the winter, for instance *Cotoneaster horizontalis*, the fishbone cotoneaster, has a mass of bright red fruits from the autumn through to February or March; in many situations the leaves also colour bright red in autumn. *C. cornubia* is a graceful deciduous shrub, strong growing to 20 ft., with a profusion of red berries in drooping clusters. The flowers are white. *C. salicifolius fructu-luteo* is evergreen, and has yellow berries; *C. disticha* has orange fruits lasting until spring and is a smallish shrub with semi-evergreen leaves and small, pinkish-white flowers. Pruning is not required except to keep them in shape or to remove crowded or weak shoots.

Decaisnea A shrub from China, *Decaisnea fargesii* reaches about 10 ft. in height with large pinnate leaves and drooping clusters of yellow flowers. Its chief attraction, however, is the deep blue, bean-like pods hanging in clusters in autumn. Inside the pods is a kind of jelly-like substance in which the seeds are embedded. The pods last a long time and are not attractive to birds. Pruning is not required.

Pernettya The first requirement of these low-growing shrubs is acid soil. Given this, they will grow well and produce their attractive berries in abundance. As evergreens they are natives to moorland conditions, and make good ground cover, and the various forms of

Pernettya mucronata have clusters of fat, round pink, white, red, lilac or deep purple berries. They require a pollinator, and the type plant *P. mucronata* can be used for this. White flowers are produced in spring. No pruning is required.

Skimmia The name for *Skimmia japonica* is taken from a Japanese word 'skimmi', and the shrub itself is a handsome slow-growing evergreen, with a rather stiff, sculptured habit of growth, its white flowers appearing in spring, followed by clusters of prominent red berries which last through the winter. Skimmias mostly have male and female flowers on separate plants, so it is necessary to have at least one of each sex to ensure berries. *S. japonica* is the commonly grown species; *S. j. fragrans* is a sweet-scented male form. *S. reevesiana* does not require a pollinator, since it is self-fertile; it has crimson, oval-shaped berries. Pruning is not required, except to tidy the bushes, and acid soil in a sunny place is preferred; however, they can be grown quite successfully in light shade and a neutral soil.

Viburnum *Viburnum davidii*, whose white flowers appear in June, has bright turquoise-blue berries, not very large but very thickly clustered, in autumn. The growth is dense and compact, and its shiny, wrinkled, evergreen leaves are another attraction. Height 2–3 ft. *V. betulifolium* is a viburnum with a quite different habit of growth, being rather loose and arching, and reaching 10–15 ft. In autumn it has masses of brilliant red berries in clusters, following the white flowers of June. It is deciduous. *V. opulus* flowers in May and June. Its red translucent berries, like luscious red currants, persist long into the winter. It also reaches a height of 10–15 ft. and is deciduous.

For other fruits, see also berberis page 8, garrya page 25 and mahonia page 27, under flowering shrubs.

(Top)
Passiflora caerulea **Constance Elliott, with beautifully-marked white flowers, is a climber for a warm wall. The orange-coloured fruits are only borne in very warm sunny summers**

(Bottom)
***Solanum crispum autumnale*, with lilac-blue flowers, is another plant for a warm, sunny wall**

(Top)
The chaenomeles or japonicas, grown for their flowers, give a bonus in the decorative fruits which can be used to make quince jam or jelly. Shown below are the fruits of *Chaenomeles cathayensis*

(Bottom)
Skimmia japonica makes a broadly dome-shaped bush of 5 ft. The large, scarlet berries are borne only on female plants

(Top)
The berries of *Viburnum davidii*. These are turquoise-blue in colour

(Bottom)
Viburnum betulifolium, one of the best of all berrying shrubs. It is deciduous

(Left)
The free-berrying forms of *Pernettya mucronata* make splendid ground-cover plants - but only on acid soils

(Right)
The bean-like pods of *Decaisnea fargesii* always draw admiring glances. They remain on the branches for an extended period

(Below)
Skimmia reevesiana (syn. *S. fortunei*) is an admirable shrub for winter colour, the berries lasting throughout the winter

CHAPTER FIVE

shrubs for small gardens

For people whose gardening is perforce on a Lilliputian scale, it is still feasible to grow small shrubs which, like their larger relatives, provide colour and beauty, and require little aftercare. Use them as individual specimens in a rock garden, in a mini mixed border or to add attraction to a sunny, paved corner in the town garden. Even more useful, they are easier to grow successfully in all sorts of containers, from the modern, shallow circular pot to the equally modern (but apparently old) Italian lead urns and tanks. Such containers fit in well to the tiny paved garden where there is often only a small area of soil available for a gardener's planting activities. Further, there is the charm that these tiny shrubs have in their own right; there is a fascination in growing exact but tiny replicas of, for instance, the Lawson cypress, or the purple-leaved *Berberis thunbergii atropurpurea*.

Of the shrubs already described the following are all on a small scale: calluna, caryopteris, *Convolvulus cneorum, Cytisus kewensis,* erica, *Genista lydia, Euphorbia* species, *Hypericum calycinum, Mahonia aquifolium* and the *Philadelphus* Manteau d'Hermine. Some other small-growing shrubs are described in the following paragraphs.

Cistus and helianthemum are both low-growing members of the *Cistaceae*, the former reaching about 3–4 ft., the latter less than a foot. Both come from the Mediterranean region and require warm positions on sharply-drained soil. If they can be protected from severe cold weather and given the sunniest position in the garden, they will produce flowers in profusion throughout the summer. The rock roses (cistus) can be obtained in white, pale pink, rosy-pink or purple varieties, and have open, saucer-shaped flowers about 3 in. across; the evergreen foliage is greyish-green. In the variety Pat, to 4 ft., the white flowers with maroon blotches can be as much as 5 in. across; Silver Pink, 2½ ft., is a lovely hybrid; *C. crispus* has mauve-red flowers and is fairly hardy; *C. corbariensis* is white and one of the hardiest, to 3 ft.

The sun roses (helianthemums) have much smaller flowers but are produced with great abandon so that they cover the plant, in yellow, red, orange, crimson, white and all shades of these colours. Alice Howarth is a double, mulberry-crimson variety; Bengal Rose is a distinctive colour break; Ben Mhor, orange; Firefly is scarlet and Wisley Primrose, yellow. Flowering is mostly in May and June.

There is a miniature version of *Berberis thunbergii*, called *B. t. atropurpurea nana*, to 2 ft., with orange flowers in spring, purple leaves and red berries later. It has the virtue of no thorns. *B. buxifolia nana*, 1½–2 ft., is a slow-growing evergreen with yellow flowers and purple-blue berries; the evergreen *B. irwinii* and any of its varieties has yellow-to-

The very large flowers of *Cistus* Pat, white with a maroon blotch, make it one of the most impressive of all rock roses

The rather tender *Artemisia arborescens*, suitable for a warm position, adds lightness and grace to a shrub or mixed border

(Top)
For warm positions where the soil is sharply drained, there is often a place where the gay summer-flowering rock roses can be grown, like *Cistus crispus* shown here

(Bottom)
Vinca minor, a less-rampant periwinkle with excellent qualities for ground cover in addition to its value as a decorative flowering plant

orange flowers and rather dark green leaves. It reaches 3 ft. but its varieties are much smaller growing.

Ceratostigma willmottianum has dark blue, phlox-shaped flowers in late summer and autumn, on a low-growing bush to about $3\frac{1}{2}$ ft., and makes a graceful and airy plant. It has red-tinted foliage in autumn. It needs protection in winter, being cut right down to the ground by frost, but will recover to break again in the spring. It will grow in sandy or heavy soil, doing rather better in the former; it is happy in an alkaline or acid soil.

Andromeda polifolia compacta is a plant for acid soils containing peat or leafmould. It reaches about 8 in. and has flowers like pink lilies-of-the-valley and rather greyish, evergreen leaves. It does well in light shade. *Ceanothus thyrsiflorus repens* is an evergreen, semi-prostrate form, between 2–3 ft. with Cambridge-blue flowers in May. It spreads eventually to cover an area of about 8–10 ft. There are attractive low-growing cotoneasters, too – for instance *C. dammeri* which will spread out over the ground and is studded with white flowers in spring, and bright red berries in autumn. The leaves are evergreen. It will grow in light shade or sun and any soil.

As regards low-growing shrubs with pleasing foliage, there are *Euonymus fortunei*, hedera, *Phlomis fruticosa*, salvia, senecio and skimmia, already mentioned. Another species of phlomis, *P. chrysophylla*, is an unusual form of the Jerusalem sage with dull gold, felted leaves, but it does need shelter from the cold, and north-east winds.

Artemisia abrotanum has light greyish-green, feathery foliage; it retreats below ground when the temperature falls but, with luck, may survive the winter. It grows to 3–4 ft., and has no flowers of any moment. *A. arborescens* is another silvery-grey foliage plant but is rather tender and really does need a warm position for it to thrive.

(Below)
Ceratostigma willmottianum forms a shrub of 3 ft., with rich blue flowers from July until autumn, when the leaves turn a bright red

(Top)
One of the attractive blue-foliaged rues, *Ruta graveolens* Jackman's Blue

(Bottom)
Pachysandra terminalis, a first-class ground cover plant for shade

Ruta graveolens Jackman's Blue is an interesting sub-shrub to 2–3 ft. Its bright blue, dissected leaves are outstanding in the border. It has yellow flowers in summer which can be left on the plant but lessen the quantity of foliage produced. *Santolina chamaecyparissus nana* is the lavender cotton, with grey-white foliage reduced to rather needle-like proportions, but plenty of it so that it is effective in the mass. Its height is 1 ft. and its bright yellow flowers appear in July. It is evergreen.

For ground cover, *Pachysandra terminalis* is an evergreen shrub little more than 6 in. tall with a variety *variegata*, with white margins to the leaves. These are excellent ground cover plants for shade. It will reach 8 in. at most. *Salix repens* is a prostrate willow, and its variety *argentea* has greyish, felted leaves. It eventually reaches about 4 ft., but takes its time over doing this, and produces a sort of miniature hummock.

The periwinkles are delightful. So often they are not allowed to show what they can do if they try, but are put in heavily shaded situations and poor soil, which is either dry or lacking in food. If given a good start in life their rambling, ground-covering shoots will travel over a large area, and produce their usually blue flowers throughout the summer in considerable numbers. *Vinca major* is the common one – and its variety *variegata* has its evergreen leaves marked with creamy-white. *V. minor* is less rampant and has blue flowers, but in its varieties they may be white, purple, sky-blue or plum. The variety *aureo-variegata* has yellow blotches on the leaves, and those who like such variegations will find this an attractive little shrub.

Other ground-cover shrubs mentioned earlier are berrying pernettya; hedera, and the heathers calluna and erica which, with judicious selection, will provide flowers most of the year, and give you attractive foliage.

shrubs for hedging

Besides serving a purely ornamental purpose shrubs have a considerable utilitarian value in their use as hedges. Moreover, it is now realised that a hedge need not be simply a long line of green in summer, and a long line of brown in winter; it can have all sorts of colours if flowering shrubs are used and it can be evergreen, thus increasing its attraction both in quantity and quality.

One may want a thick, strong hedge to provide shelter and privacy at all times of the year – an evergreen like holly, yew or cupressocyparis would be suitable. Perhaps the hedge is required only for dividing one part of the garden from another. For this escallonia, fuchsia or spiraea are all good. One should further consider whether it is to be formal or informal, i.e. clipped to a rigid, smooth outline, or allowed to grow more or less as it pleases, removing the odd errant shoot only. This method of training suits the flowering hedges best.

Planting is carried out as a general rule from autumn through to spring for deciduous hedges; for the evergreens September–October or March–April are the best times. If the weather is at all dry after planting, water well in the evenings, particularly the evergreens, and spray the latter with clear water every day. Cold, strong winds can also cause moisture loss through the leaves and in such weather extra water may be needed.

Soil preparation

Preparation of the soil before planting is extremely important, and the same methods apply as are mentioned on page 52. Dig in as much organic matter as possible – this is vital, since the hedge is going to be such a permanent feature and it is rather difficult to improve the soil satisfactorily after planting. This soil preparation particularly applies to privet which is a heavy feeder.

Prepare the soil several weeks in advance and then, when the shrubs arrive, dig out a trench of such a width and depth as will take the roots comfortably without cramping. Where long hedges are concerned, it will be found easier and more convenient to do the planting section by section, digging out a short length of trench at a time, and heeling in the plants temporarily until actually planting. Staking a hedge is not necessary.

Trimming hedges

The tools to be used for cutting and trimming may be shears, secateurs, loppers or mechanical electrical trimmers. For hedges consisting of plants with rather large evergreen leaves, such as laurel, secateurs should be used; shears will cut the leaves which then die back and may result in the plant growing badly or dying. Secateurs can also be used where an informal hedge is being trained, merely to cut out untidy shoots here and there.

Instructions for training and clipping hedges after planting, as part of the routine aftercare, are given in the list of plants which follows, but as a general rule cut all deciduous hedges back to 9–12 in. high in the spring after planting *unless* they are spring planted; privet and *Lonicera nitida* are two evergreens which can also be cut back, but on the whole evergreens should be left alone after planting.

Routine cutting is done at least once a year, but the top of the hedge is allowed to grow, and is not clipped until the height required is reached. Training the top of a formal hedge to the correct shape is important; it should be flat, roof-like or rounded, with the base broader than the top, and the sides sloping. This ensures that snow, wet and general debris do not collect in the top. This might seem a small matter but snow in particular can be a menace, as the weight of a heavy fall can break quite sizable branches and spoil the symmetry of the hedge.

(Opposite page)
Berberis stenophylla, a shrub which makes a splendid evergreen screen and provides welcome colour in spring

(Below left)
The popular japonicas (chaenomeles) make a useful screen from spring until the leaves begin to fall in autumn

(Below right)
Cotoneaster simonsii, associated here with golden privet, ***Ligustrum ovalifolium aureum***, is another popular, attractive hedging shrub. The berries often persist right through the winter

HEDGING SHRUBS

Key   D: Deciduous   E: Evergreen   F: Flowering

Plants	Planting distance in feet	Cut back after planting	When to trim	Height in feet	Remarks
Berberis buxifolia nana EF	1–1¼		After flowering	2	Yellow flowers in early spring
B. gagnepainii EF	1½		After flowering	5–7	Yellow flowers in May
B. stenophylla EF	1½–2		After flowering	8–10	Deep yellow flowers in spring
B. thunbergii atropurpurea Rose Glow DF	1¼–1¾	9–12 in.	February	6–8	Orange flowers in spring. Young shoots rose-coloured
Buxus sempervirens (Box) E	1½–2		In summer	9	
B. s. suffruticosa E	4 in.		2–3 times in summer	3	Used for edging
Carpinus betulus (Hornbeam) D	1¼–1¾	Not for 2 yrs	July	10–20	
Chaenomeles (Japonica) DF	1–1½	9–12 in.	Early May	2–10	Red, pink or white flowers in spring
Chamaecyparis lawsoniana E	1½–3		August		Fast growing; varieties *allumii*, glaucous-blue; *fletcheri*, bluish-green; *stewartii*, golden
Cotoneaster dielsianus DF	1½	9–12 in.	March	6–9	Spring flowering, red berries and autumn leaf colour
C. lacteus EF	1½–2		March	12	Red berries
C. simonsii DF	1–1½		March	12	White flowers in May, red berries, semi-evergreen
Crataegus monogyna DF (Hawthorn, Quick)	¾–1¼	6 in.	June or as required	5–20	White flowers in May, red berries
Cupressocyparis leylandii E	3–4		July–August	10–15	Grows 2½–3 ft. a year, suited to coast
Escallonia Apple Blossom and C. F. Ball EF	1–1½		Late summer	5–6	Specially suited to seaside gardens
Escallonia macrantha EF	1–1½		Late summer	4–10	Rose-crimson flowers in June, glossy foliage, suited only to mild districts and seaside

Plants	Planting distance in feet	Cut back after planting	When to trim	Height in feet	Remarks
Fagus (Beech) D	1¼–1¾	Not for 2 yrs	Early August	5–10	Copper beech has purple foliage
Forsythia intermedia spectabilis D	2–3		After flowering	6–8	Large, deep yellow flowers profusely borne in early spring
Fuchsia magellanica riccartonii DF	1–1½		Spring	3–8	Red and purple flowers in June–October, plant 4 in. deep. Can be damaged by cold weather; suitable for seaside gardens
Hebe EF			April	2–5	Late summer flowering, hardy and half hardy
Ilex (Holly) E	1½–2		Late summer	5–20	Plain and variegated leaves, red berries
Laurus nobilis (Sweet Bay) E	1½–2		August	10–20	Use secateurs; good in shade
Lavandula (Lavender) EF	1 or 2–2½		After flowering	1–4	Plant spring; July–August flowering; do not cut into old wood
Ligustrum ovalifolium (Privet) E	1	9 in.	May, September	2–10	Variety *aureum*, the Golden Privet, is popular
Lonicera nitida E	1	9–12 in.	2–3 times in summer	4–4½	
Metasequoia glyptostroboides D	2	9–12 in.	3–4 times in summer	5–10	Damp soil; pink foliage in autumn
Osmarea burkwoodii EF	1¼–1¾		April	9–12	Fragrant white flowers in spring
Pittosporum tenuifolium E	2		April	10–20	Tender, good at seaside
Potentilla fruticosa DF	1–1½	9–12 in.	Early spring	5	Yellow flowers in summer
Prunus cistena DF	1	9–12 in.	After flowering	5–7	White flowers in spring, purple leaves
P. laurocerasus (Laurel) E	1½–2		April or early August	5–20	Use secateurs
Pyracantha (Firethorn) EF	1½–2		April	6 or more	White flowers in spring, red, orange or yellow berries; use secateurs
Rhododendron ponticum EF	1½–2		Remove dead flowers	8–15	Acid soil. Purple flowers in June
Rosmarinus (Rosemary) EF	1–1¼		April	3–4	Plant April; blue flowers June, aromatic grey leaves
Spiraea DF	1–2	9–12 in.	Early summer or March	4–5	White or pink flowers in spring or summer
Taxus baccata (Yew) E	1–2		August–September	10–15	Grows 1–1½ ft. a year
Thuya occidentalis E	1½–2		Late summer	5–12	
Viburnum tinus (Laurustinus) EF	1½		April	6–10	White and pink flowers in winter
Weigela hybrids DF	2–3	9–12 in.	After flowering	6–9	White, pink or red flowers in early summer

(Top)
The hardy *Hebe* Autumn Blue, a variety which makes an attractive informal screen. Some of the more tender kinds can be used for hedge-making in coastal districts

(Bottom)
Few shrubs equal the hollies as hedging plants, nor adapt so readily to widely-differing conditions. In time, they form an impenetrable screen. Shown here is *Ilex* Silver Queen

(Top)
The old-world charm of lavender makes it a popular choice for forming a low internal division in the garden

(Bottom)
Another shrub which makes an attractive low screen is *Potentilla fruticosa* Tangerine

(Opposite page)
A veritable 'wall' of colour is provided by a hedge of the tall-growing *Pyracantha atalantioides*

choosing and planting shrubs

Shrubs can now be obtained in three different ways: from the specialist shrub nurseries by ordering, in sealed packs from the chain stores, and from 'garden centres'.

Ordering from a nursery
Until recently the only way to buy shrubs was to place an order for them in spring or early summer, about six months before planting. This was because the nurseries started lifting their plants from the end of September onwards, to send them out through autumn and early winter so that the customer could plant them before really cold or wet weather arrived after Christmas, and while the soil was still comparatively warm from the summer. It is still advisable to order shrubs in the early summer, otherwise, with orders taken in strict rotation, the plants may not arrive until the following spring.

Polythene packs
However, during the last few years, shrubs have also become available in sealed polythene packs at chain stores, ironmongers, and garden sundriesmen. Plants for these packs are lifted, shoots and roots trimmed, leaves removed (to prevent water loss from the pores or 'stomata' of the leaves), roots wrapped in moss and polythene and the whole plant sealed into a polythene wrap, so that it remains fresh for a long time. The pack is convenient to handle and carry, and if the ground is not quite ready for planting, the plant can be left in its wrap without having to be heeled in to await planting.

Containers
A third method has also recently developed in that nurseries have started to grow their shrubs in disposable containers. One can now drive direct to the nursery concerned, look round it and decide what is wanted, and take away one's choice there and then. The plant suffers a minimum of disturbance, planting can be undertaken at a time convenient to the buyer and, provided it is done carefully and the plant given the appropriate aftercare, can be carried out at any time of the year, except obviously under extreme weather conditions. These container-grown plants are sold at the 'garden centre' type of nursery, of which there is now a growing number.

PREPARATION OF SOIL
One might wonder why it is that plants have roots and grow in soil at all; in fact in some tropical countries they grow on the bark of trees, or in mountainous districts on stones where there does not seem to be any soil. However, the answer lies, not in the soil itself, but in the plants' method of feeding.

Although green plants get the bulk of their sustenance from the air in the form of carbon

(Top)
Dig a bed if the shrub is to be planted in a lawn. Loosen the bottom soil and add compost to this

(Bottom)
Make a mound of soil in the centre of the bed and rest the roots on this. The soil mark on the root ball is level with the lawn. Spread the roots out

(Top)
Return the soil, with added compost, to the hole. Shake the shrub so the soil particles filter round the roots

(Bottom)
Firm the compost during the planting but do not tread so heavily that the soil becomes compacted. Smooth the soil and tidy up the surrounding area

dioxide, they also need other substances, and these are usually called the plants' food.

In the case of most plants grown in this country, they get their food and water from the soil. Not only this, they must have most of their food in liquid form, and this is provided in the form of dissolved substances in the soil moisture. This moisture is absorbed into the plants' roots by a special process known as 'osmosis' and will only work if the liquid already in the plant contains more dissolved substances – not necessarily the same ones – and is more concentrated than the liquid outside the roots. If the reverse happens, and the soil moisture is more concentrated, the liquid in the roots is drawn out, the roots become dried up and do not work properly, and liquid in turn is drawn from the part of the plant above the ground to replace that lost from the root. The process goes on until eventually the leaves begin to show signs of drying up, or desiccation, which in its extreme form takes the appearance of browning round the edges of the leaves and withering.

This is why it is so important, when feeding plants – particularly with concentrated 'artificial' fertilisers – not to apply more than the recommended quantity.

Another reason for planting in soil, at any rate in this country, is that it serves as an anchor for the plant. It is possible to grow a good many plants in a solution of liquid nutrients only, but they will always require a support of some kind if this is done.

It should now be much more apparent how important the roots are, and how vital it is that they should be treated correctly when planting, and also how necessary it is that the soil is prepared properly beforehand.

There is another point which is of importance when considering soil, and that is what is known as its structure. The way in which the soil particles stick together, and what these particles consist of, is of great importance in determining whether a soil has a poor or a good structure. One in which clay particles predominate is known as a heavy soil, if only because it tends to retain water to a very considerable extent, and it may be grossly lacking in air.

A sandy soil, on the other hand, is loosely put together – the chemical nature of the grains of sand is such that they are easily separated, so that water drains quickly through the soil taking plant foods with it.

There are soils containing sand and clay to varying degrees between the two extremes, and the ingredient which helps to modify them to a certain extent is 'humus'. This is rotted organic matter, such as leafmould, garden compost, farmyard manure or anything of a vegetable or animal origin. Humus helps the sandy soil to retain water and food; conversely, in the mainly clay kind, it improves the air content and alters the way in which the clay particles are bound together so that water is able to drain through it satisfactorily.

One essential point to remember, when deciding where to plant shrubs, is to allow sufficient space for their ultimate height and spread, whether they are planted singly in borders with other plants, or grouped together in their own borders, or singly in grass. It is heartbreaking – and can be back-breaking too – to have to dig them up and transplant them after a few years, because they are crowding everything else out or are doing badly from lack of room.

By then it is more than likely that all the available space has been filled in the garden, and the ruthless destruction of the shrub, or some other plant, is necessary. Do make sure of their height and spread first, and allow space accordingly. If this means large empty spaces for a while, they can always be filled in with annuals, or herbaceous perennials with short lives, or with bulbs and bedding plants.

(Opposite)
Ceanothus Cascade, an aptly-named variety. Like other evergreen ceanothus it needs the protection of a wall as it is rather tender

(Top)
The exquisite blooms of *Camellia williamsii* Donation are of the choicest of their kind and of unusually beautiful colouring

(Bottom)
Rhododendron fastigiatum, one of the smaller-growing species. The flowers are carried prolifically in April and May

Digging

If possible, the place where the shrub is to be planted should be dug over to a depth of one spit (one spade deep) and the bottom of the hole covered with a layer, about 3 in. deep, of well-rotted compost, farmyard manure or leafmould. This is forked up and mixed with the soil at the bottom of the hole which can then be left, if need be, for a little while. Make sure that perennial weeds have been carefully and thoroughly removed.

PLANTING

When the shrub arrives, have a good look at the roots, and if any are broken, cut them so that they end cleanly and not in a jagged finish, which might rot or become infected with a soil disease. Do the same with the top growth, cutting back any broken or dying shoots to just above a leaf joint. The inside of a dead shoot is brown when the bark is scraped away with the thumb. If the shrub needs a support, and they mostly do while they are getting established, put a stake into the hole first, making sure that it is quite firm.

It is a good idea to have somebody to help with planting, if only to hold the shrub in position while the soil is replaced around it. A shallow mound in the centre of the bottom of the hole enables the roots to spread out more easily and point slightly downwards, which they would do naturally. Spread the roots out so that they extend comfortably to their full length, and put the plant in at such a depth that the soil-level mark stained on the stem from the time it was growing in the nursery is level with the top of the hole, and then add soil mixed with more compost or peat, shaking the plant at intervals, so that the soil particles filter down between the roots. Do this until the hole is half full, then firm it with the heel and add more soil to bring it up to the level of the surrounding ground. The addition of a little bonemeal, about a handful, thoroughly mixed with the soil when planting, will help the roots to get going.

Tie the shrub securely to the support but not so tightly as to constrict the stem; a piece of sacking round the stem will protect it from chafing. Allow for slight sinking of the shrub as the soil compacts. Tidy up the surrounding area, and rake over the topsoil lightly, so that the surface is broken up. If smooth, this tends to prevent the water seeping down, and encourages the growth of moss. If planting in a lawn, make a small square or circular bed round the shrub and keep this free of weeds while the plant is getting established.

Moisture loss

If planting evergreens or conifers in the spring, dry weather or strong cold winds could occur. This results in rather a pronounced loss of moisture. As the foliage is still on the plant, it will be losing moisture by 'transpiration' through the stomata, at a time when the roots are not growing and absorbing liquid, so it is advisable to spray the top growth over every day, with water, in order that the stomata may remain closed and prevent this loss of moisture; also one should make sure that the soil is really moist deep down as well as on the surface. A special compound is available to spray on to the leaves which seals them so that transpiration does not occur. This eventually washes off and does no harm to the plant, and some shrubs are in fact sent out with this already applied.

Watering in the average shrub after planting is unlikely to be necessary, except where the soil is already dry, when heavy watering beforehand, and regular watering afterwards while the weather remains dry, will be required. Never plant in dry soil and make sure that the ball of soil round the roots of plants from pots or other containers is thoroughly moist before starting the planting operation.

caring for shrubs

One of the nicest things about shrubs is the very small amount of regular aftercare they require from the gardener.

AFTERCARE

Mulching every springtime – which means adding a layer of material to the surface of the soil round the plant – is virtually all that is needed, apart from pruning, and occasional feeding with a proprietary fertiliser.

The mulch should be several inches thick, placed around the plant in an area that will cover the probable spread of the roots. In practice this is at least equal to the spread of the branches, but if this is rather large, it need not be strictly adhered to. Garden compost, leafmould, peat, spent hops, mushroom compost and very well-rotted farmyard manure can all be used, and will help to improve the structure and drainage of the soil and supply it with food, which is generally washed into the soil by rain. Be careful not to get the mulch too close to the base of the stems as it could provide a cosy home for mice and voles, who will chew the bark of the shrub and so kill it.

Feeding

The addition, occasionally (say every two or three years) of what is known as a concentrated or 'artificial' fertiliser, which contains the most necessary of the chemicals essential for the plant's diet, can be helpful in producing a first-class plant, particularly where it is growing on soil which contains a good deal of sand. Water drains through such soil quickly, and as the chemicals are dissolved in the water, naturally the plant foods are also lost. (Mulches on these soils act as sponges and help to retain water and food.) If fertilisers are to be given, the spring is the time to do it. Bonemeal may be used in the autumn.

Lime-hating plants

In some of the descriptions of shrubs it is mentioned that they require an acid soil; if an attempt is made to grow them in alkaline soils the leaves turn yellow and growth stops unless special steps are taken. Most people grow only those shrubs which are suitable to their soil, but sometimes they consider special treatment is worth while. A simple soil tester will show if the soil is alkaline, and if it is, lime-hating shrubs must be started off in a pocket of lime-free soil. This of itself is not enough, and the shrub must be watered once or twice a year, according to the degree of alkalinity of the soil, with a solution of a proprietary chelate or Sequestrene compound. This can, however, be quite expensive over the course of years.

PRUNING

Many shrubs, if unpruned, rapidly deteriorate into flowerless, straggly plants, full of leaf, with crowded stems and lots of 'birds' nests'. Pruning encourages the production of new shoots which will have flowers on them and, when done in conjunction with regular mulching and occasional feeding, will produce healthy attractive plants. The removal of crossing shoots, diseased shoots or those that are too close, can be carried out; this is important as it lets air into the centre of the bush, and also light which ripens the flowering buds and ensures a better display the following year. Broken branches should be removed by cutting cleanly back to a suitable junction. If the branch is very big, the wound made by cutting should be painted with a sealing compound or grafting wax, to prevent the entry of diseases.

Technical terms

The explanation of one or two terms used in pruning might be useful. 'Cutting back to a bud' means cutting off the shoot with a clean cut in such a way that the cut is made just above the part of the stalk where a leaf or a pair of leaves grows out of the stem. Between the leaf stalk and the stem will often be found a small bud which may be a flower bud, or a vegetative bud – the sort of bud which grows into another shoot. The cut is made above this bud, taking care neither to damage nor to remove it. It is important to make a clean cut.

'Tipping' means cutting off the young growing shoot, removing only about 2 in., possibly 3 in., from the top of the shoot. Cutting 'hard back' means removing most of a shoot, about three-quarters of it; or hard back may mean almost to ground level.

Pruning 'lightly', or 'thinning' means either removing about a quarter of each new shoot all over the bush, or removing an occasional shoot entirely, simply to prevent overcrowding.

Tools

For most pruning, a pair of secateurs is all that is needed, either with a blade cutting down on to an anvil, or the scissor type. A knife is also sometimes useful, and a pair of lopping shears or branch cutters for removal of rather large, tough shoots.

Time to prune

The majority of shrubs fall into two classes so far as pruning is concerned: those which flower from July onwards and are pruned in the spring in March, and those which flower

(Left)
Hardy varieties of fuchsia are becoming more and more popular with gardeners. Here they are seen in association with honeysuckle, *Alchemilla mollis* and liatris

(Opposite page, top)
Buddleia alternifolia, a distinctive species which makes a handsome small tree when trained as a standard. It flowers in early summer

(Opposite page, bottom)
Shrubs and stone paving are always a happy association, the beauty of foliage textures being as important in most cases as the delights of floral colour

from the spring until the end of June and are pruned immediately after the flowers die.

The late-flowering shrubs are pruned in March when the plant is starting into growth, to stimulate the production of lots of new shoots which will carry flowers later in the season. The spring flowerers, pruned immediately after flowering, should normally have the old flowering shoots cut off, except where the fruits are attractive. They should either be cut back to strong new shoots which will already be growing to take their place or, if these have not yet started, to within an inch or two above the base of the old flowering shoot; this may be to ground level.

Where special pruning is required this is mentioned with the description of the shrub concerned. Some may only require the removal of the dead flowerheads as with rhododendrons; straggling shoots may need tidying.

With judicious pruning, not necessarily every year, it is possible to produce the maximum of flower and yet preserve or enhance the natural habit of the shrub.

PESTS AND DISEASES

Another point about the ease of aftercare of shrubs is that they suffer, on the whole, from relatively few attacks by insect pests or fungus diseases. Always follow manufacturer's instructions when using chemicals.

Aphids The ubiquitous greenfly, or the blackfly (both are aphids) feed on the tips of young shoots, especially where they are particularly soft and succulent; they may be liquidated with derris, malathion, nicotine (which is very poisonous) or by squashing with the finger and thumb.

Leafminers Leafminers sometimes attack shrubs, particularly holly. These can be difficult to deal with but rarely occur in great numbers; use a systemic insecticide containing dimethoate which is absorbed through the leaf, or taken up by the roots.

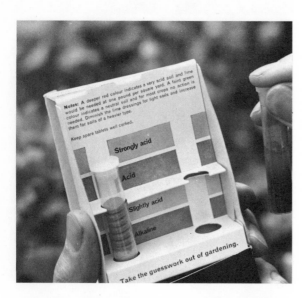

Caterpillars Caterpillars, if there are enough of them, warrant the use of malathion.

Capsids Capsids sometimes produce pinholes in the leaves, particularly on the tips of young shoots; treat as aphids.

Vine weevil Rhododendrons, azaleas, and occasionally other shrubs may be attacked by the vine weevil adult, which bites semi-circular holes in the margins of the leaves. Attacks mostly occur on leaves near the ground. Control is difficult, but dusting with BHC may help, and spraying the ground to kill the larvae again with BHC may also help.

Honey fungus There are one or two diseases which may cause trouble. Where a shrub starts to die for no apparent reason and is not old, the fungus disease known as honey fungus should be suspected. This has toadstools the same colour as honey, with round, flattish caps, and they can be found growing at the base of trees or shrubs. They do not appear, unfortunately, until the plant attacked is dead, and the only other way to diagnose the trouble is to dig in the soil around the base of the shrub and at some distance away from it. Thick black threads like bootlaces will be found running close to the roots of the shrub concerned. Even when diagnosed, it does not help a great deal since it is unlikely that the plant can be saved, but at least one will know that the ground is contaminated, and no more woody plants should be grown in that spot. Control by the amateur, other than wholesale removal of the soil from the spot, is not possible yet. Leaving dead stumps of shrubs and trees in the soil encourages this fungus, and they should be removed.

Silver leaf Shrubs are occasionally attacked by silver-leaf disease, a fungus which more commonly occurs on plum trees. The name aptly describes the greyish-silver effect which overlies the natural green of the leaves. In some cases the disease dies out of its own accord, in other cases it is necessary to cut off

(Top)
Removing frost-damaged tips on a forsythia, an attention which many shrubs need in spring

(Bottom)
Pruning a variety of *Buddleia davidii* in March. A pair of long-handled secateurs, or loppers as they are sometimes called, are invaluable where larger growths have to be dealt with

(Top)
Trimming half-ripe cuttings of *Weigela florida variegata* before insertion

(Bottom)
The weigela cuttings inserted round the edge of a small pot in a sandy rooting compost

the attacked branch. Any wood killed by silver leaf must be cut out and burned.

Canker Canker sometimes occurs – the stems become swollen and knobbly and later the bark cracks in a circle round the stem, which then dies from the canker to the tip of the shoot. Cut back to a bud in healthy wood and burn the diseased part. This disease often occurs where the climate is damp.

Scab Apple scab may occur on shrubs related to the apple family, the *Rosaceae*, but spraying regularly with captan as instructed by the manufacturer will control it.

Mildew Mildew may occur on leaves; this is a white powdery meal and can show on stems as well as leaves; dinocap will control it.

PROPAGATION

The production of new plants is a subject which can fill a book in its own right, and there is sufficient space here only to touch on the outlines, but for those who would like to try it, the following will suggest ways which can be studied later in greater detail.

Plants in general, not shrubs specifically, are propagated either by seed or by vegetative means. If grown from seed, the resulting plant will be a totally new one, with some of the characteristics of each parent or earlier ancestors, resulting in a mixture different to any that has previously appeared. Seedlings of natural species are usually much like their parents, but seedlings of hybrids and garden varieties seldom are. If grown by vegetative means, the plant will be exactly the same as its parent, and these methods of propagation include taking cuttings of various types, using rooted layers, suckers and runners, division of the parent plant, grafting, and budding (which is a form of grafting).

(Left)
A deciduous berberis hybrid giving a bright display of autumn colour. These useful shrubs have many roles to play in modern gardens

Seeds

Propagating shrubs from seed can be rather a slow business since it may take some years for the seedling to reach an appreciable size. The seeds should be collected as soon as ripe and stored dry in a cool dark place through the winter. If one of the berry type, they should be placed in layers in shallow moist sand out of doors during winter, provided they are hardy, as this makes eventual germination quicker.

Sow the seeds in spring in either a standard seed compost or the sort of soil in which the shrub normally grows, space out the resultant seedlings and transfer to permanent positions after two or three years.

Cuttings

Half-ripe cuttings of shoots are taken in July–August, using the current year's shoots, provided they have not flowered. These are of the kind beginning to harden at the base, close to the parent stem. They should be 2–6 in. long, with the lower leaves cleanly removed, and should be placed in a sandy compost, or moist silver sand, protected by glass in a box or frame, out of doors in a lightly shaded place. Keep the rooting medium moist and when the cutting has rooted, put it into potting compost and grow on as usual.

Hardwood cuttings are taken in October–November from current year's shoots which are fully ripened, and in which the stem is hard and woody all the way up. These cuttings are up to 12 in. long, and are treated in the same way, but can be rooted out of doors directly into the soil with a little silver sand at the bottom of the hole. The cutting is buried for two-thirds of its length and left over the winter, protected if the weather is very cold. When rooted it is transferred to a permanent position the following autumn.

The production of roots on cuttings, whether half-ripe or hardwood, can be hastened and increased by the use of hormone rooting powders, available at various strengths according to the type of cutting.

Layering

Layering of some shrubs is another method. The tip of the stem is placed on the ground in a shallow hole, and bent sharply upwards so as to form a U-shape. It is pinned down in this position and covered with soil. The autumn is the best time to do this, or the spring, and rooting should have occurred by the following autumn. Cutting the shoot a little at the bend, below a leaf joint, will encourage the production of roots.

Germination of seed and rooting of half-ripe cuttings may be encouraged by placing them in an electrically operated mist spray in a greenhouse.

COMMON NAMES AND THEIR BOTANICAL EQUIVALENTS

Barberry – berberis
Beech – fagus
Box – buxus
Broom, Common – cytisus
Broom, Mount Etna – *Genista aethnensis*
Cotton lavender – santolina
Firethorn – pyracantha
Fishbone cotoneaster –
  Cotoneaster horizontalis
Hawthorn – crataegus
Heath – erica
Heather – calluna
Holly – ilex
Honeysuckle – lonicera
Hornbeam – carpinus
Ivy – hedera
Japonica – chaenomeles
Jasmine – *Jasminum officinale*
Jessamine – *Jasminum officinale*
Lad's love – *Artemisia abrotanum*
Laurel – *Prunus laurocerasus*
Laurustinus – *Viburnum tinus*
Lilac – syringa

Lavender – lavandula
Mile-a-minute vine –
  Polygonum baldschuanicum
Mock Orange blossom – philadelphus
Orange blossom, Mexican – *Choisya ternata*
Passion flower – passiflora
Periwinkle – vinca
Privet – ligustrum
Quickthorn – crataegus
Rock rose – cistus
Rosemary – rosmarinus
Rue – ruta
Russian vine – *Polygonum baldschuanicum*
Sage – salvia
Sage, Jerusalem – *Phlomis fruticosa*
Southernwood – *Artemisia abrotanum*
Spindle tree – *Euonymus europaeus*
Spiraea, Blue – caryopteris
Sun rose – helianthemum
Sweet bay – laurus
Tamarisk – tamarix
Tree lupin – *Lupinus arboreus*
Vine – vitis
Willow – salix
Winter sweet – *Chimonanthus praecox*
Witch-hazel, Chinese – *Hamamelis mollis*

Acknowledgements

The author gratefully acknowledges the help received from the following in illustrating this book: *Amateur Gardening*, Robert J. Corbin, Ernest Crowson of J. E. Downward, Valerie Finnis, A. J. Huxley, May & Baker Group of Companies, Elsa M. Megson, The Murphy Chemical Co. Ltd., R. V. G. Rundle and Harry Smith.

© The Hamlyn Publishing Group Limited 1970
SBN 600 44175 X
Published by The Hamlyn Publishing Group Limited
London · New York · Sydney · Toronto
Hamlyn House, Feltham, Middlesex, England
Phototypeset by Jolly & Barber Ltd, Rugby
Printed in Hong Kong by Dai Nippon